PROFIT
SECRETS
REVEALED

Profit from Knowing What Your Accountant Knows... But Doesn't Tell You

MATT JULL

Published by My Business People

Auckland, New Zealand

Copyright © 2014 Matt Jull

The moral right of the author has been asserted.

ISBN: 978-0-473-27638-6

AUTHOR ONLINE!
For a free online course and more resources, visit
www.ProfitSecretsRevealed.com

Profit Secrets Revealed

DEDICATION

Firstly to my late father Boyd, who was my first teacher on this topic. To my wife who is both an accountant and critic of this work. For my four boys, I hope that you too will be inspired to one day join the ranks of those with an entrepreneurs spirit (after you've completed your studies). To my many clients, past and present who I respect and admire for your own commitment to your businesses. My wish for you all is that you continue to experience greater successes in your endeavors. And lastly to you the reader, I dedicate this book and hope that you may prosper in your business career.

CONTENTS

ACKNOWLEDGMENTS

This book owes its existence to my wife who suggested that I write it. I would also like to thank Barry Dow, who taught me so many lessons about business and finance. Special thanks also goes to my team of experts from around the world especially Mia Shotwell for her dedication to editing this work. Lastly, I'd like to thank Paul Wilton for his enthusiasm, support and encouragement.

1 THE POWER BEHIND YOUR BUSINESS SUCCESS

For anyone entering the world of becoming the owner of a business, they will find that it can be confusing, frustrating and at times isolating. For those who are already business owners, they will have experienced this at one time or another.

In the past, I've felt this way myself and have since met many other business owners who have told me of the same struggles. I can totally relate to many of the heart-breaking experiences and frustrations felt all over the world by entrepreneurs just like you.

In small business, we all have a number of people we can turn to for wise council and advice. Most often we turn to our spouse or life partner, as well as other family members and friends. Sometimes, but less often, we may seek guidance from our accountant, bank manager or lawyer.

Many owners of businesses don't feel that they have received good advice from their professional advisors. This is a sad fact that I've encountered many times. Oftentimes they quite honestly didn't understand the advice they received and revert back to asking family and friends, or worse, not asking for help at all.

Unfortunately for many business owners, they seek advice from the wrong people. If this is you, then I'd like to make it very clear right here, right now – **it's not your fault**.

I don't say 'it's not your fault' to give you any excuses or ways of escape from any mistakes you've made in the past. What I mean by this statement is that it has been my personal experience and ongoing observation that most business owners are in business for themselves because they have some specialty or technical skill to offer. During the years of learning and honing their technical skill or area of specialisation, they were most likely never taught how to run a business.

In fact, I'm yet to meet anyone who was ever taught anything of value about how to run a successful business in the trades, technical school, or even university. Learning to run a business is only achieved at the foot of a mentor. Some, like me, have had that good fortune. Others, however – and probably the majority – have not.

Before we go any further in this journey together, I'd like to make one thing very clear – I am NOT an Accountant. What I am is someone who has been trained to be a Great General Manager of my own businesses.

I started my business career after finishing an

apprenticeship in the construction industry and, like many others with a set of skills who started their own business, I started my first business because someone wanted to buy my skills. It was in the early 1990's and there was nothing except my trade that qualified me to own a business – sound familiar? I learnt very quickly that I needed help. I therefore turned to anyone and everyone who I knew, or even just had met, and asked one simple question "how do I grow my business?"

While some of the advice I received was useful, there wasn't anyone with a structure, plan or the time to help me put all the information into some sort of order and give a path to follow until I met my first mentor. This person was just what my business and I needed at that time. They put structure and accountability into place and called me every week to hold management meetings over the phone. We discussed the results from the previous week and set new plans in place for the next week. This person was in effect teaching me how to become the General Manager of my own business.

It is now my privilege to do the same for many other business owners from around the globe. I've included some of the methods that I teach every week to my clients in this book.

My methods are simple really; first you need to know that there are four key building blocks in your business that you must master. In order, these are: Finance, Sales & Marketing, Systems and People.

With any of the businesses I'm working on, I always start with financial mastery. The two main reasons for this are : profit and cashflow. More profit and cash are powerful stress relievers for any business. Financial mastery for a business owner is knowing what, out of everything you do or sell, is one: most profitable and two: the most cash abundant.

With greater profit and more cash, you can focus more attention on sales and marketing campaigns, especially those that show the greatest returns – I'll tell you more about this later in the book.

As you begin to generate more profit and cashflow, you can then begin to invest in system and equipment upgrades, to leverage greater efficiencies in your business. Then you must hire and train excellent people to operate these systems and equipment.

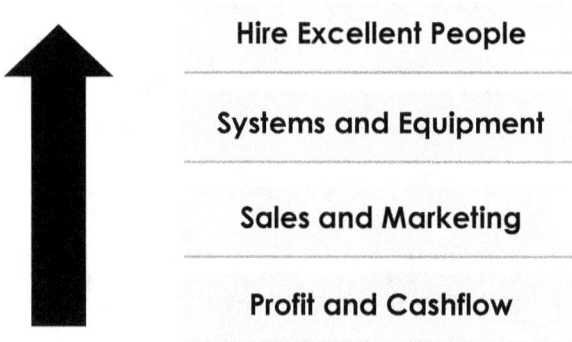

| Hire Excellent People |
| Systems and Equipment |
| Sales and Marketing |
| Profit and Cashflow |

Matt's Path to Business Success

The first step towards success in business is learning how to master the decision-making power that lies behind understanding your financial management reports. Financial mastery or your profits and cashflow is the foundation building-block, as well as the purpose behind this book. In it you will learn the basics about profits and cashflow in order to become a Great General Manager of your business.

2 YOUR NUMBER ONE RESOURCE

Well you actually have two great resources available to you that will help you on your journey to grow a successful business. The first resource is implementing and properly using a computer-based accounting software system in your business – did I just hear you groan with disappointment? The second resource is creating a strong line of communication with your accountant – there's the second groan.

The first, using an accounting software system, isn't as hard as it might seem, nor does it need to be expensive. A word of caution here: do your research and find a system that works for your business.

There are many accounting systems in the market, that may or may not work for you. I've met many business owners who have invested good money into software that is incompatible, out of date, and lacks good support from the suppliers. Many are just cashbook systems – also known as single-entry accounting, and will not produce quality management reports that we will discuss later in this book.

There are many things to consider before investing in your accounting software.

Bryan and Jane are a brother and sister team. Jane has been instrumental in helping Bryan who is the owner of the business. Jane took over the role of bookkeeping and administration – this was by his own admission, not Bryan's forte so he was happy to have Jane assist him.

When I first met Bryan and Jane, I could see very clearly that they were overwhelmed by the paper war they had created, as well as using a complex accounting system without the formal training to do so.

One of the early wins in this business was to simplify the accounting system and move the business over to Xero, a cloud-based accounting program. The time savings alone were extraordinary. What used to take Jane all day to reconcile now only takes about an hour. Jane now has more time to work on other areas of the business.

- Is it simple to use?
- Was it created for accountants or business owners?
- Is it cloud-based or local server based?
- Does it seamlessly integrate with other software like point of sale, billable time logs or inventory management?
- What sort of support is offered?

- What type of businesses are using it and how many?
- Does my accountant use the Accountants version?
- What sort of reports can I generate from it?
- How many user licenses come with the package?

Before choosing an accounting package, ask your accountant for any suggestions, go online and research what's available, and ask others in your industry what they are using.

It's about here that most people ask me what accounting software I use. Well it's not so much what I use that's important, but what I recommend for small businesses. I've used many different accounting software packages over the years some of which were very expensive and hard to use unless you were an accountant and they are now in the bin.

As I understand it and, from what I've experienced, the history behind the development of many accounting software platforms is that they were designed specifically for accounting practices and big businesses. The developers then realised that there was another market, the SME or Small to Medium Enterprise market. They took their complex software developed for professionals and stripped it down to make it marginally more user-friendly or navigable. As a result, accounting software was still too complex for most business owners to get their heads around. Most of the time, they didn't use its full functionality and opted on using the invoicing function to look professional in front of their customers. Sometimes they didn't even use it at all. Either way, it would never produce accurate reports of any real value to the business owner, unless it was kept up-to-date with its data entered in full

In the current age, we have some superb software programmes available that were designed especially for SME business owners and are very easy to use.

I often recommend Xero to many SME business owners because it is low cost, easy to use, and cloud-based. Xero provides regular and secure, automated feeds from their bank, makes reconciliations incredibly simple, cuts down on time to enter data, and can be integrated with a good range of other useful software applications. Since it is cloud-based, you can grant access to other parties who view or work on your accounts for you. Many business owners have taken this option and get great service from either a bookkeeper or their accountant who doesn't even have to step foot into their office to do the books.

Action Points

- If you're not using an accounting software system, then get one.
- If your current software isn't a double-entry accounting system and doesn't produce proper management reports, such as Profit and Loss and Balance Sheet, then it's time to upgrade your system.

Your Other Number One Resource

As I mentioned in the first section of this chapter, it is vital that you develop strong lines of communication with your accountant. I know the title of this book might suggest that they are privy to some amazing secrets, and maybe they have been holding out on you. The truth is your accountant is your number one advisor in a lot of major decisions about your business – and some of the minor ones, too.

I've met a lot of business owners who never really tap into the wealth of knowledge that their accountant holds. I believe there are many reasons for this, but mostly it's because they don't really know when they should, or why they should ask for advice. In many cases, this has led to feelings of frustration or confusion about their accountant's role in the business and ultimately, they become reluctant and disgruntled clients.

If you don't have a great relationship with your accountant but you would like one, then let me share with you one of the key principles behind becoming a success in everything that you do. This is the first thing that my mentor taught me and now I teach it to everyone I meet. It is the principle of Above The Line.

As a successful business owner, I have the Responsibility to take Ownership and be Accountable for everything that happens in my business. This is my Above The Line attitude. A Below The Line attitude would be the complete opposite response, including Blaming others, making Excuses and living in Denial. Below the line is like a silent killer that slowly rots away at the foundations of everything that you attempt to build.

So as a business owner, I choose to live my life and run my business Above The Line. I invite you to choose the same path. If you are prepared to follow this path, then the responsibility for having a great relationship with your accountant lies with you. The first step is to say out loud the following statement:

"I choose to live my life Above The Line and take Responsibility for all my business decisions, be Accountable to follow through on my decisions and take Ownership of any of the results both good and not so good".

As a helpful reminder, I also recommend that you make a copy of Above The Line Principle and stick it on a wall somewhere where you'll clearly see it from your desk.

OWNERSHIP

ACCOUNTABLE

RESPONSIBLE

BLAME

EXCUSE

DENIAL

How To Get The Best From Your Accountant

What does my accountant do? It has always been my experience that the accountants I've met genuinely want the best for their clients and their businesses. Equally, I've met a lot of people who get great advice from their accountant, but I probably meet more people who are in some way disappointed with their accountant. If you fall into the latter, let's first look at what an accountant does for you.

To answer this question, you first need to understand that there are two types of accounting professions. The first is called Financial accounting and the other is called Managerial or Cost accounting.

Without getting too technical, financial accounting is accounting that focuses on providing historical information to people outside of the business, such as government agencies and your bank manager. Managerial accounting provides real-time, analytical information to people inside the business like yourself, the business owner who is acting as the general manager. This information helps you make informed decisions about the future strategies that you may decide on for the future success of your business.

So, getting back to the question of "what does my accountant do?" If your accountant is in private practice, then they most likely have a degree in accounting from university, plus have invested another 3-4 years to fine tune their financial accounting knowledge through the chartered accounting institute. They are mainly responsible for producing annual financial statements for your business and presenting these statements to the government agency who wants to collect your taxes.

If you are relying solely on these annual financial statements to see how your business is performing and make decisions based on the past for the sake of your future, then you could be in for a whole world of trouble. By the time your annual accounts are prepared, they will be so horribly out of date that they will offer little to no help in making major decisions that benefit your business. In fact, statistics that I have seen show that business owners who rely only on these annual reports to make financial and strategic decisions about their business have just a thirty six percent chance of survival – Whereas, businesses that report monthly have a seventy nine percent survival rate.

Now, please don't think that what I've said should be a negative slur on your accountant's participation in advising you about your business. Remember it is your responsibility to press into building a great relationship with them, and their advice and service is of great importance to you and your business.

But what is equally important is that you must learn to understand how to read the reports that relate to financial accounting, as well as the reports developed inside your business that relate to managerial accounting. Your chances of success will increase if you read these reports at least monthly, instead of annually. Your accountant is the one person who can teach you the most about your business's financials and how to successfully interpret what the numbers tell you.

To get the best out of your accountant, you should arrange regular contact with them, and be organised because accountants sell time. The more organised you are, the less you'll pay. Think through in advance what you need to discuss and achieve in your meeting. In this case, communication is essential, so send them an agenda and ask them what information they are going to need you to provide. Make sure you have this agenda ready in advance. If you employ a bookkeeper take them with you to a few meetings to make sure they are able to ask questions they may need answers to, like how to correctly allocate expenditure.

Here are some things you should ask your accountant:
- How does my business compare with my competition? Do you have any bench marking information to support

this?

- Is my gross profit margin reasonable for my type of business and how can I improve it?

- Which of my products or services are making me the most profit?

- How can I reduce my expenses without compromising my quality or service?

- What can I do to improve my cashflow?

You'll notice in these questions that I never once asked how to reduce my tax bill. All too often I find that's the biggest question people ask their accountants. In my view, it's the WRONG question – don't worry, I've made the same mistake too.

Jason, the owner of a construction business, has developed an amazing line of communication with his accountant. When I first met Jason, he was typical of many business owners who never thought to meet with their accountant more than once a year.

Jason says "Some of the early advice Matt gave me was that successful business owners have many advisors. He encouraged me to meet more often with my accountant, Paul. For over a year now, I've been meeting with Paul every four weeks, and he has been of immense help to us".

If your focus is constantly on how to reduce costs and save taxes, you'll never crack a profit of any real significance. Focus instead on increasing profit margins. We'll discuss increasing sales a little later in this book.

Final Word (in this chapter)

The financial accounting reports that your accountant produces mostly relate to just two reports: your profit and loss report and your balance sheet. From here on in, I will refer to these as your management reports.

In the next chapter, I will get into more detail about management accounting reports, of which there are many. I'm going to keep to the basics and discuss pricing, simple performance measures, cash flow and budgeting in the coming chapters.

Action Points

The three things I am going to do to improve about my relationship with my accountant?

1.

2.

3.

If there is one thing I'd really like to ask my accountant, what would it be?

---

3 PROFIT AND LOSS (P&L)

Now that you've invested in an accounting software solution, and you've gotten some up-to-date data, you can start generating your monthly management reports, starting with your Profit and Loss statement, shown in Table 1.

This report is a fantastic tool. The measurements for your businesses performance start here. It's not just about the profit that you make, or where your money is going on your expenses.

There are five main components to your P&L:

- Sales
- Cost of sales
- Gross profit
- Expenses
- Nett profit.

These are split into two parts, top line and bottom line. You would have heard of the "bottom line", but you've maybe not heard of your "top line". Your top line is the money you've made after you've deducted your costs of sales from your sales, which leaves you with your gross profit. Your bottom line is commonly called your nett profit and is the actual profit you've made after deducting your expenses from your gross profit.

Table 1

Profit and Loss Accounts for ABC Ltd
12 months ended 31 March

	2011	2012	2013
Sales			
Labour	650,000	550,000	350,000
Materials	480,000	380,000	450,000
	1,130,000	930,000	800,000
Cost of Sales			
Contractors	360,000	260,000	400,000
Materials	340,000	210,000	250,000
	700,000	470,000	650,000
Gross Profit	430,000	460,000	150,000
Expenses			
Accounting	5,000	5,000	5,000
Advertising	10,000	15,000	12,000
Bank Fees	1,500	1,500	1,500
Depreciation	15,000	12,000	10,000
Insurance	25,000	25,000	22,000
Interest	15,000	15,000	15,000
Office Supplies	10,000	10,000	10,000
Power	20,000	25,000	25,000
Rent	30,000	30,000	30,000
Telephone	15,000	20,000	20,000
Vehicle expenses	35,000	30,000	30,000
Wages	115,000	120,000	120,000
Total overheads (fixed costs)	296,500	308,500	300,500
Net Profit / loss	133,500	151,500	-150,500

Now I want to add a side note here, and this may be another reason why many business owners find looking at their accounts and listening to their accountant a confusing experience. There are many different words used for sales, cost of sales, gross profit, expenses and nett profit. For instance, sales are also called turnover or income, expenses can be called fixed costs, operating costs, or overheads, and nett profit can be called nett income or simply profit.

There also many abbreviations like COS, GP, EBIT and EBITDAR, so if it all sounds like gibberish, please remember this is an opportunity to step above the line and ask your accountant what this all means. You will in time, grow accustomed to accounting jargon.

Table 2

Profit and Loss Accounts for ABC Ltd
12 months ended 31 March

	2011	2012	2013
Sales			
Labour	650,000	550,000	350,000
Materials	480,000	380,000	450,000
	1,130,000	930,000	800,000
Cost of Sales			
Contractors	360,000	260,000	400,000
Materials	340,000	210,000	250,000
	700,000	470,000	650,000
Gross Profit	430,000	460,000	150,000

Back to your P&L, let's start with your top line. In Table 2, you will see that there is a bit of a breakdown of what the sales consisted of and what the cost of sales consisted of. For example, the cost of contractors corresponds with the sale of labour. We'll come back to the level of this breakdown in a moment because it's an important part of your reporting.

Working Out Your Top Line (Gross Profit)

To work out your gross profit, (GP) you simply deduct the cost of sale from your sales.

Sales – Cost of Sales (COS) = Gross Profit (GP)

Or as in this Table;

$1,130,000 – $700,000 = $430,000

Working Out Your Gross Profit As A Percentage (Margin)

The most powerful number to know from your P&L is your gross profit margin. (margin) The right information will allow you to quickly calculate them as a percentage.

To work out your margin, divide your gross profit by your sales.

Gross Profit (GP) ÷ Sales = Margin

Or with the numbers from the P&L

$430,000 ÷ $1,130,000 = 0.380

By moving the decimal point, (0.380) you'll get 38%. This is the average margin for this business during that period of trading. It gets interesting when you find out where the higher and lower margins come from in the business. You can start making decisions about where to focus your attention to increase your margins and build a more profitable business.

Let's go back to the break downs of the sales and cost of sales. The income from labour was $650,000 and the cost of labour (contractors) was $360,000. The formula above leads to your gross profit.

$650,000 - $360,000 = $290,000

With a gross profit of $290,000, you now need to work out the margin (remember the formula? Gross Profit ÷ Sales = Margin)

$290,000 ÷ $650,000 = 0.446

Move the decimal point and you've got 44.6%. For this business, that might be a good margin on labour in the industry that they're in, but the key here is to make more profit. Where can we look to increase the profit in this business? Let's look at the materials.

The gross profit of materials is...

$480,000 - $340,000 = $140,000

And the margin is...

$140,000 ÷ $480,000 = 0.291 or 29.1%

If the margin on labour is 44.6%, then the margin of 29.1% on materials is pulling down the overall margin to an average of 38%.

As the business owner, you can put your general manager's hat on and start looking for ways to increase your margins. The starting point is getting a good break down of your sales and the cost of your sales. This is where I like to have more details in my P&L.

Imagine for a moment a building company, they might include more detail like labour cost (wages), materials, equipment hire, sub-contractors, freight and rubbish disposal. A retailer carrying hundreds or thousands to units of goods might categorise them into different lines and report those categories. The point is, having good quality information in your P&L and knowledge about your margins is a powerful starting point. Begin focusing more of your attention on what is profitable and what isn't.

Now it's time for you to get a bit practice. Get a pen and work out the margin for 2012 and 2013 (refer to Table 1):

	2011	2012	2013
Sales	$1,130,000		
Gross Profit	$ 430,000		
Gross Margin	38%		

Working Out Your Bottom Line (Nett Profit)

The next part of your P&L deals mostly with your expenses. These are sometimes referred to as your fixed expenses. The word fixed is used because they are expenses that you will have regardless of whether you make any sales or not. These expenses must be accounted for and the bills paid like rent, power, phones and wages.

It is important to keep track of and control your expenses, but if you spend too much time trying to control the expenses, you won't make any major impact on increasing your profits. Instead focus your energy on increasing your margins because that is the secret to gaining your maximum potential for profits.

It's also where I see business owners going off on a tangent and trying to reduce their taxes. As a word to the wise, this will take you away from making more profit.

There are a bunch of tools that will help you control your expenses, including cashflow forecasts and budgets, which I'll go into more detail soon.

To work out your nett profit, it's just a simple matter of subtracting your expenses from your gross profit

Table 3

Gross Profit	430,000	460,000	150,000
Expenses			
Accounting	5,000	5,000	5,000
Advertising	10,000	15,000	12,000
Bank Fees	1,500	1,500	1,500
Depreciation	15,000	12,000	10,000
Insurance	25,000	25,000	22,000
Interest	15,000	15,000	15,000
Office Supplies	10,000	10,000	10,000
Power	20,000	25,000	25,000
Rent	30,000	30,000	30,000
Telephone	15,000	20,000	20,000
Vehicle expenses	35,000	30,000	30,000
Wages	115,000	120,000	120,000
Total overheads (fixed costs)	296,500	308,500	300,500
Net Profit / loss	133,500	151,500	-150,500

Gross Profit – Expenses = Nett Profits

Or as shown here in the 2011 column

$430,000 - $296,500 = $133,500

Alex, the owner of a home renovations franchise, has experienced some rapid growth. This year, his business has tripled because he has good systems for reporting his sales, work in progress, cashflow and profit ratios. He has been successful in controlling this growth.

"Every Monday morning, we meet with our team of builders and review every stage of where sales and work in progress are at. This has helped me build a sense of team, as well as security with the guys. My wife and I also have regular management meetings with Matt and together we review our monthly P&L, along with some other reports.

Matt always pushes me to increase my margins. We know through bench marking that we are well above the industry average. While it's been stressful at times, I believe that if we didn't have our level of reporting, I doubt we would have stayed in control of our growth".

Takeaways From This Chapter

- Review and compare your P&L monthly
- Know your margins on everything
- Focus on your margins to build greater profitability into your business
- Control your expenses, but not at the expense of increasing your margin (focus big, not small)
- Margin, margin, margin

4 MARK UP VS MARGIN

Two terms used when discussing pricing your product or service are markup and margin. These are different ways of calculating profit, and the difference can be confusing. I am still constantly amazed when I meet with business owners and ask the question, "what are your margins?" and they reply by telling me their mark up instead. If you are someone who doesn't understand the difference, then it's like I said at the beginning of this book, "it's not your fault". No one has taken the time to explain the difference to you. Thankfully you now have this book in your hands, and together we can set the record straight.

First let me make it very clear that mark up is NOT the same as margin. Knowing the difference will help you set your pricing strategies more effectively and ultimately help you make more money.

If you are marking up your prices by let's say thirty percent, then please don't be fooled into thinking that you are making thirty percent because you're not. For instance, a margin of thirty percent will give you more cash in your hand than a mark up of thirty percent. You'll see this in the examples below.

Mark up is, as the name suggests, the percentage of value that you increase your product or service by.

Cost of Sale x Increased Percentage = Mark Up

Whereas margin is the percentage of gross profit that you make on the sale of your product or service. The two are never the same number. Recording mark up does not give you the same type of decision-making power like the information that comes from tracking and measuring your margins.

This will start to make sense once we look at the numbers, let's take an item that you sell for $100 and say that your cost of sale is $70 Your gross profit will be $30 or a 30% margin (30 divided into 100 is .3 or 30).

Now if you mark up the $70 by 30%, you won't get $30. Let's quickly work that out.

$70 x .3 (30%) = $21

This would make your sell price $91 instead of $100, and what's worse, is it only works out to be a 23% margin ($21 ÷ $91 = 23%). So how do you work out what the mark up is if you need to make a 30% margin?

The formula is like the reverse of how you would work out your margin.

Gross Profit ÷ Cost of Sale = Mark Up

Let's take the original sale price of $100 from which we know the cost of sale is $70. When we subtract the two, we get a gross profit of $30. The above formula gives you a mark up percentage of 42.8%.

$30 ÷ $70 = 42.8%

Here's another way to look at how mark up and margin work

$30
Gross Profit

Mark up
42.8%

Margin
30%

$70
Cost of Sale

$100
Sale Value

This is a powerful formula to know for market research. If

you already know what your cost of sale is, you'll have a good idea that your competitor's costs will be about the same as yours. If you know what they are selling their products for, by using this formula you'll be able to get a good idea of what their mark up is.

A Simple Way To Mark Up By Margin

Your business might be the type that sells its products directly from a supplier's price list. You are constantly adding a mark up to the price list. Rather than always having to back cost to make certain that you are making the right margin, there is simpler way to work it out:

For a 5% margin, divide the cost price by 0.95.

For a 10% margin, divide the cost price by 0.9.

For a 15% margin, divide the cost price by 0.85.

For a 20% margin, divide the cost price by 0.8.

For a 25% margin, divide the cost price by 0.75.

For a 30% margin, divide the cost price by 0.7.

Hopefully, you can see the pattern. Here's a quick reference table for you to use:

Desired margin   Divide cost price by

5%	.95
10%	.9
15%	.85
20%	.8
25%	.75
30%	.7
35%	.65
40%	.6
45%	.55
50%	.5
55%	.45
60%	.40
65%	.35
70%	.30
75%	.25
80%	.20
85%	.15
90%	.1
95%	.05

For a 100% margin, the cost price would have to be zero.

Takeaways From This Chapter

- Mark up and Margin are not the same
- Mark up is the percentage of money that you increase the price by
- Margin is the percentage of Gross Profit from the sale

5 DISCOUNTING DISASTERS

It seems to me that a lot of business owners are heavily involved in discounting just to get the sale. I believe this comes from two areas, the first being that it is common practice in some industries to use loss-leading or discount-related advertising to attract customers. This mostly happens in the retail of Fast Moving Consumer Goods (FMCG). FMCG are products like food or grocery items that have a short shelf life and are often advertised heavily to call customers to take action and buy. This blanket marketing has tricked many other business owners from completely different industries into thinking that in order to get more customers or get the customer to buy from them, they have to give a discount. Nothing could be further from the truth.

The other reason a lot of SME business owners and their salespeople give discounts is because no one has taught them to sell properly. The key to good sales, or as I call it professionally allowing customers to buy, is that you must understand your customer's perception of value for money and why they should buy from you. Often a customer is motivated to buy for completely different reasons than just what the price is. One example of this is someone who wants some work done on their home. This is a completely emotional sale. The customer is always emotionally invested in their home, and their biggest concern is always the same: "Can I trust this person coming into my home?" Now, if trusting you is their biggest concern, then why would you offer a discount? It makes more sense to give them good reasons to trust you, rather than offering a cheaper price.

I found this out first hand when in the late 1990's, I started a tile business. By the early 2000's, we had worked out that trusting us was the number one motivating factor in seventy eight percent of our customers' buying decisions – only three percent said it was price. We started to give them good reasons to trust us by being highly responsive with all our communications. If we said we would do something, we made sure it was done. We had a policy of under four hour replies to phone calls and emails. We also gave our quotes within 24 hours and turned up on time. If we were running late, even if by only five minutes, we would call and let them know we would be late. We told them that they can trust us on all our marketing material. Even our tag line said, "tilers you can trust". The upshot of all of this was that we started to put our rates up, and by the time I sold that business in 2003, our base rates for tiling were thirty eight percent more expensive per square metre than the industry average at the time. In fact, as I sit here and write this book, the tile industry has only just caught up to the match the same square metre rates we were charging 10 years ago.

Discounting is and always will be disastrous to any SME. I hope that my own experience inspires you to stop discounting and take another, more profitable path. If you're still not convinced, then let me show you how dangerous discounting can be for your business. Think of something that you normally sell for $100. Let's say that the cost of sale is $70 on that item, so your gross profit would be $30. If you discount that $100 by 10% making the new price $90, how much are you giving away in dollar value? This would be $10 of the sale. But what have you really done?

	10% Disc	**33% Less GP**
$30 GP	$20 GP	
$70 COS	$70 COS	
$100 Sale	$90 Sale	

This is where the reality of discounting gets interesting. Only $30 of that original $100 was yours. By giving what most would consider a tiny discount of only 10%, you are now left with just $20. You have in fact given away one-third of your money. What does this mean to you? You have just given away 33% of your gross profit and now you have to work three times harder and sell three times more to get back to where you started before you gave that tiny discount.

What other costs would that incur? If you discount, you will now add more costs to your business because you now have to work harder and sell more. These costs may include additional staff hours, freight or power, more money tied up in stock, interest, and all sorts of other costs. Now let's really, really drill down to make this really hurt and make you want to cry.

If your sales are one hundred thousand dollars every month and your gross profit is thirty thousand, a ten percent discount on every sale will add up to one hundred and twenty thousand dollars every year that you are giving away. That's more than a month's sales, even worse that's four months of gross profit you are giving away every year

If you are discounting to make a sale, you've got to stop and make some positive changes in your business and consider this. What if you increase your prices? Let's take a look at that same scenario

What if you increase your price by 10%? The sale price would now be $110, but your cost of sale would still be $70. Your gross profit increases by raising the price. In fact, your gross profit would increase by 25%. Your business would be a lot healthier, and you would be enjoying the benefits of increased cash in your hand.

25% More GP

$30 GP | $40 GP

$70 COS | $70 COS

$100 Sale | $110 Sale

What's more, if your dollar sales decreased by 25% you wouldn't lose any money. In other words, if you're still concerned about how your customers would react to you putting your prices up by just 10%, you could take a dip in your dollar sales by up to 24.99% and still make more money than you did before putting your prices up.

6 OVERCOMING RESISTANCE TO PRICE INCREASES

If you are thinking to yourself, like I've heard many people say, "my customers will walk if I increase my prices" then I ask you this: is that an Above The Line attitude? Let's be truly honest. Who is the biggest resister to change in your business? Is it you, your staff or maybe your customers? As an owner of a successful business, you have to always be ahead of the bell curve of change. Those who resist it will have change forced upon them and it might be too late for them.

Like in my story about my tile business, the answer was simple. We asked our customers for feedback about why they bought from us and not our competition. We then made it easy for them to decide to buy from us by giving them what they wanted. The key is to find out now and make the right changes before someone or something makes those changes for you.

Some years ago, I was involved in helping a business make these changes that had come about because the government had forced the changes on all the businesses in the country. That change was an increase in the minimum wage. This business was a chain of Asian grocery stores. The owner Patrick had, by his admission, gotten side-tracked with other business ventures and community work, and the business had suffered and was showing little return. With around two hundred employees, many who were part-time and on minimum wage, Patrick was faced with an increased wage bill of about one hundred thousand dollars. When we looked at different ways of covering this increase in wages, it was clear that because of the time constraints with the changes to the minimum wages being just a month away, the quickest way to address the problem was to raise all the prices on all the items in the stores by ten cents.

Now apart from my wife having a great grandfather who was of Chinese descent, I had had very limited dealings with people from China. When I told Patrick about this strategy, he fired straight back at me with stories about how his customers loved discounts. In fact, if he advertised soya sauce for one cent cheaper in one of his stores, he would get car loads of Chinese housewives driving across town, past three or four of his other stores along the way, just to save that one cent.

I quickly learnt that the Chinese have a reputation for being the most price-sensitive people on the planet. They pride themselves on their negotiation skills and love getting a discount. But the fact remained, the government was pressing on with this change that was now being forced of Patrick's business. He therefore conceded and agreed that it must be done my way.

Later that week, Patrick and I met with his store managers and we broke the news to them. The price on every item in every store must be increased by ten cents. I will never forget the look of horror on the faces of each manager. Needless to say it was a tough meeting, but eventually the respect that the mangers had for Patrick prevailed, and prices were put up the next day.

Three days later I had a panicked Patrick on the phone: "Matt, they didn't put the prices up ten cents, they put them up **ten percent**." The mangers had totally misunderstood us. As it turned out, English was their second language and Patrick, as a fifth generation Chinese Kiwi, spoke no Chinese. Now we understood why there had been so much resistance at the meeting. My first response was that this was excellent news, but Patrick was very concerned about losing his customers. After some discussion, we agreed to wait and see what happened. Long story short, Patrick didn't lose any customers. In fact, the sales in the stores increased, and over the coming year, he not only covered the increase in wages, but made a handsome profit.

While we were lucky enough to save this business from disaster, history is littered with many industries and businesses who have closed down because they didn't respond soon enough to change. Remember to embrace change, put up your prices and stay ahead of the bell curve.

Six Sure Fire Ways To Get Your Customers To Pay You More

- Survey your customers and ask them why they buy from you and what frustrates them about your industry.
- Tell your customers why they should buy from you, use a tag line or unique selling position and offer guarantees that take away their frustrations.
- Put your prices up
- Make a three-option close e.g. teach your sales team to give a three-options cheapest, mid-range and most expensive deal, instead of only offering the cheapest deal.
- Re-write your quotes into Plans of Action – most quotes look like an invoice and don't give your customer any reason to buy apart from price. In a Plan of Action, tell them more than just the price and give them reasons to buy from you, instead of the competition.
- Have scripts for overcoming objections such as, "Apart from price, is there anything else that would prevent you from buying today?"

Create A Point Of Difference – Retail

If you are in retail, it is important to realise that everyone else in retail is offering the same thing, discounts. The market place has become extremely noisy and consumers are more and more underwhelmed by discounting. The key for you is to identify what it is that your customers want the most, many will say service is the answer.

While this may be true, the first step in your journey is to ask you customers why they shop with you, take time to listen and then observe how they react in your store. Creating a point of difference is far more than saying service is the key, the real answer is held in the expectations that your customer has of being served.

Use Written Communication To Educate Your Customer

Every time you communicate with your customer in written form, you have an opportunity to educate them on why they should purchase from you and not your competition. All your communications, at a minimum should include your tag line, and where possible include your guarantees. These will reinforce in the mind of your customer, the reason why you are the better choice and minimise the effect of competing on price.

One of the most under utilised forms of communication is your quotation form. Quotes are often mistakenly thought of as simply a way of giving someone the costs to do a job, if your customer requests a price and all you give them is a standard looking form, then you've missed a massive opportunity. In fact a standard quote form can be very damaging to the relationship, because most standard forms look similar, if not exactly like an invoice. This gives the appearance of invoicing for the work, before the customer has accepted the quote.

If you're involved in quoting for work then I strongly advise that you re-write your quotes into Plans of Action.

On the next page you will see that I've included a sample of how a standard quote form looks, and how similar it is to an invoice. There is very little information on it other than price for the customer to decide on.

Following that I've included a real life Plan of Action, this is the exact template that I used in my tile company, not only did it help me increase my conversion rate, it also communicated to the customer why we were their best option and justified our more expensive rates (our base rates were thirty eight percent higher than the rest of the market).

Example of a traditional quote form

DESIGN
L O G O

Great Job Building Co

Quote No.

QUOTE

Customer		Misc	
Name		Date	
Address		Order No.	
City	P code	Rep	
Phone		FOB	

Qty	Description	Unit Price	TOTAL
100	Of these things	$ 1.00	$ 100.00
220	Of these as well	$ 25.00	$ 5,500.00
15	And you'll need some of these too	$ 3.20	$ 48.00

		SubTotal	$ 5,648.00
		Shipping	
		Discount -10.00%	$ (564.80)
		Tax 15.00%	$ 847.20
		TOTAL	$ 5,930.40

Payment Other

Comments
Name
CC #
Expires

Office Use Only

Payment due on the 20th of the month following invoice (but we know you won't pay on time, but that's ok because the bank will bail us out with a nice fat overdraft)

Thank you

Example of a Plan of Action

MTC

tilers you can trust
PO Box 151-066
New Lynn
Telephone   09 817-2332
Facsimile   09 817-5527
Email   mob.tile@ihug.co.nz

Include your *Unique Selling Position* in every communication and make sure it addresses the customer's biggest concern about dealing with your industry

Quote #

Date

Name
Address
Ph
Email

Never miss an opportunity to upsell the customer by adding more value

Get the money question out in the open first use the word *investment or value*, never called it cost or price

Good morning / afternoon, Name

Thank you for taking the time to consider carefully the installation of your tiles. I enjoyed discussing your requirements when we last met and I am certain that you will absolutely love the results.

Your investment is just $------- [incl GST], complete ... installed and guaranteed. And for only $115.00 you are able to take advantage of our unique 5 Year Peace of Mind Warrantee. *For further information see the section on "Chips and Cracks" on the next page.*

Payment can be made by *VISA, Master Card, American Express* or *Cheque*. A 25% deposit will be required prior to commencing the project with the final payment due on the signing off of the **Tile Contractor Inspection Certificate**.

Make it easy for the customer to buy by taking credit cards

Just to make sure that I have everything correct, your requirements are...

Add your guarantees into the scope of works

- Cover carpets with plastic wrap
- Grout and buff tiles to finish, silicone corners [grey floors / white walls].
- Remove rubbish from site.

NAME, while price is an important consideration, so to are the following points...

Give more guarantees to *de-risk* the purchase

1. MTC offer an unbeatable **3 Point Guarantee**... first, all materials we use are backed by a **Manufactures 10 Year Guarantee**. Second, our workmanship is guaranteed for a lifetime. Third, we promise you the very best service and advice.

2. Competent trades people who are Preferred Contractors to MTC and participate in our Quality Performance Guarantee will carry out the installation of your tiles.

45

**Explain the process so the
customer has confidence in you
and they know what to expect**

3. At the end of the job you can inspect the tiling with the tiler and sign off your satisfaction using our **Tile Contractor Inspection Certificate**. At this time you may also request that the tiler repair anything that maybe of concern to you.

What else makes MTC so unique?

Quality... in a word, only premium grade materials will be employed in the installation of your tiles you can be assured that we only use the very best available. It is for this very reason **you don't have to worry** about tiles coming unglued or waterproofing leaking because of poor and inferior products.

**Give even more
guarantees to
de-risk the
purchase**

Cracked Tiles... We use only the highest quality flexible adhesives; even over concrete floors and we bandage construction cuts and cracks in the slab where necessary to isolate cracks from the tiles. This may cost a little more but we do all this to minimise cracking in the time during structural movement.

Waterproofing... The Mobile Tile Company makes no excuses for being fastidious to the enth degree with this issue. After all, you do not want your house leaking or rot and mould to set in do you?
All our contractors have had extensive training by trade professionals and the manufactures of waterproofing products. A Ten Year Guarantee backs all the waterproofing products we use.

**Up sell the
customer into
another
guarantee**

Chips and Cracks... Let's face it accidents happen and buildings move with the changing of the seasons. Choose our **5 Year Peace of Mind Warrantee** for only $115.00. This extended warrantee covers removal and relaying of chipped or cracked tiles of up to 2 square metres at no extra cost to you.

NAME, I look forward to working with you to produce a tile finish that you will love and that will complement your home beautifully.

Have a great day,

**Talk directly to the customer by
repeating their name at least three
times**

Matthew Jull

PS I will phone you in the next three days to organize a convenient time to get started, or if you wish to speak to me sooner please phone me on 0800 423-884.

**Finalise the quote by explaining
the next step, this will reinforce
the customers confidence in you**

7 YOUR BIGGEST OPPORTUNITY

When looking at your expense column on your P&L, one of the biggest opportunities you have is knowing what to keep track of by consistently measuring and what to simply track as a cost of doing business. A cost of doing business will include normal fixed costs like rent, power, phone, accounts, subscriptions, vehicle operating costs, and so on. On the other hand, there are costs in your expense column that relate to investments that you've made like staff wages and training, systemisation, and marketing. These should all produce a result and therefore will be measurable.

These measures are often called KPI's or Key Performance Indicators and are measurements of both performance and return on investment. KPI's will give you greater control over your business and a greater understanding about the difference between <u>Your</u> profit and <u>Your</u> loss.

Because every business is different, each individual business's KPI's will be unique to that business. There are thousands of articles and hundreds of books written about KPI's. For many business owners, knowing which KPI's to measure in their business is often a frustration that many never resolve. Therefore, these business owners never get started with setting out any KPI's. Those who do set up ways of measuring the results in the business often give up at some point because they become too busy with the "**busyness of business**". This type of business continues along its own merry way controlling the business owner, instead of the owner controlling the business.

The key to having good KPI's in your business isn't just knowing what to measure but, also the <u>consistency</u> of doing it. Measure everything is the catch cry of consultants around the world who specialise in setting up elaborate systems for measuring the most minute details in large companies. As the owner of a SME, I prefer to keep it simple and ask myself: "which expense do I need to get a return on investment from?"

As discussed throughout this book, gross profit margins are something which you must measure. In fact, margins are indeed a KPI, as well as the costs of sale that you must measure to help control your margins like productivity, material costs, and so on. With this type of KPI, you'd be looking to minimise some form of wastage in your business. This may include labour hours lost, over-ordering, the wastage of materials, or even expired goods that must be thrown out.

Likewise, if you make an investment in creating a new position for a new staff member for your business, you'd also want to have KPI's to measure the effectiveness of both the staff member and the position they hold.

A good example of having KPI's for staff might include sales staff, or as in one client's business, an automotive repair shop run by Nick and based on Auckland's North Shore. Nick and his team repair manual and automatic car transmissions. They have three workshops and a number of technicians working for them on the shop floor. For about 40 years, this business has recorded information about what the billable hours were on every job, as well as the hours of work for each technician employed there. Nobody ever thought to consistently measure these as KPI's and track the difference between those hours worked and hours charged.

Nick, who has been doing a superb job collecting this information and recording it in a spreadsheet, is now sharing the results with all his team at their weekly meetings. Everyone is focused on making improvements. He has also done his research and found out from the Motor Trade Association that the average for his industry is that twenty percent of the hours worked are non-billable (in most businesses, it would be near impossible to bill out one hundred percent of a staff's hours).

When Nick started measuring the billable verses non-billable hours, the difference was at thirty six percent non-billable or unproductive hours. In the first month of measuring and sharing this information with his team, the change was dramatic, they went from thirty six percent to twenty six percent non-billable. That's more than a twenty eight percent improvement in performance, which has directly impacted the top line by making the business more profitable.

Now the team at Nick's workshop have a goal of beating the industry standard and has set a new performance target of fifteen percent.

The biggest opportunity in front of every business owner is to know how to get a return on their investment in sales and marketing. Most businesses blindly spend money on marketing that makes them little to no money. It's like spending $1 to lose $2, or taking a bucket of water to the desert, tipping it out on the sand and hoping to create a beautiful oasis.

Smart business owners know that if they invest $1, they'll make $2, $3 or more in return. Once they've struck this formula, they keep investing in it. They know this because they measure all their results for sales and marketing. When you start to measure the results from your sales and marketing, you'll start to see patterns emerge. These patterns will help you make better investment choices in your marketing. You will also tweak and fine tune the conversion of these leads into paying customers.

Some of the measures you will need to consider when setting up your KPI's for your sales and marketing will include the cost of the campaign (your investment), number of enquiries or leads each campaign generates, acquisition cost for each of those leads, conversion of those leads into proposals or quotes, and the number that turns into customers. You also need to consider what the average dollar value is, the average margin of those sales, and the breakeven point for that campaign (I will show you more about the power of breakeven and why it's important later in this book).

Table 4

Weekly Sales and Marketing Sheet

For the month of ...

Week ending Friday

Lead Sources	MARKETING COSTS				PRODUCT / SERVICE / CATAGORY										
	Leads Generated	Marketing Spend	Lead Acquisition Cost	ROI	Total proposals / bids / sales calls	Conversion # 1	Total new clients / customers	Conversion # 2	Average Conversion Rate	Average Dollar Sale	Total $ Sales	Margin	Gross Profit	Breakeven
Radio	6	$ 757.35	$ 126.23	750%	6	100%	6	100%	100%	$ 1,072.93	$ 6,437.58	64%	$ 4,120.05	$ 1,183.36
Referrals	8	$ -	$ -		8	100%	4	50%	50%	$ 1,250.99	$ 5,003.96	60%	$ 3,002.38	$ -
Other websites	115	$ 995.00	$ 8.65	829%	115	100%	13	11%	11%	$ 710.70	$ 9,239.10	64%	$ 5,913.02	$ 1,554.69
Website	35	$ 1,500.00	$ 57.69	1400%	33	94%	26	79%	74%	$ 865.48	$ 22,502.48	64%	$ 14,401.59	$ 2,343.75
Local Paper	12	$ 1,340.00	$ 223.33	610%	8	67%	6	75%	50%	$ 1,586.73	$ 9,520.38	64%	$ 6,093.04	$ 2,093.75
TOTALS	176	$ 4,592.35	$ 26.09	1048%	170	97%	55	32%	31%	$ 5,486.83	$ 52,703.50	63%	$ 33,530.08	$ 7,175.55

This might sound like a lot of information, or perhaps even a bit intimidating so I've made it easy for you. When you sign up for the free online course that accompanies this book at, **www.ProfitSecretsRevealed.com** you can download the same spreadsheet template, for free.

This is the same spreadsheet that I give to all my clients (like the one in Table 4). The formulas are already coded into the template and all you need to do is enter your numbers. The report will automatically work out your results so you can quickly and easily get started on setting up your own sales and marketing KPI's.

To interpret your results, you must focus on where you can get your quickest wins. As in Leo's marquee hire business, we measured the many different categories or types of customers. We then simplified the customers into two main groups: Corporate events customers and private events customers. From these KPI's, some patterns started to emerge. Leo's conversion on his Corporate customers was quite good as well as the value of the quotes he'd been putting out into the market. When we looked at the private customers, the numbers told us a different story. Like private birthday parties, for instance, we could see that the conversion was good, but the dollar value was low.

Armed with this information Leo put together package deals with lighting, heating, flooring, tables and chairs and included these deals with the marquee to lift the average dollar sale of these types of events. The numbers for another type of customer, the wedding market showed us a major opportunity. The value of the quotes for this market was more than nine hundred and ninety seven thousand dollars but the conversion, which was sitting at only sixteen percent, showed us an amazing opportunity to double or maybe triple those sales. The secret lay in the conversion of the wedding market. Therefore, his business now has a dedicated staff member just to look after this type of customer.

In this spreadsheet (Table 4) you'll see actual results that another one of my clients, Danny began to measure his marketing results, and once again, we saw two main areas for improvement. The first was in his radio advertising. On the positive side, the value of the work that radio generated is the highest value of all his marketing. The conversion from lead to quote to customer was one hundred percent (it's pretty hard to improve one hundred percent). It was the number of leads that the radio produced that was the issue. The radio was generating leads in the low digits, which compared to other marketing which generated hundreds of leads, was by contrast performing pretty badly.

The remedy lay in having a conversion with the Radio Stations Sales Representative. Radio stations don't make money from only one marketing campaign. They're in the business of holding you as a long term customer. Their Rep's will do almost anything to keep you as a customer. Danny's Radio Rep got him better time slots and reviewed the advertising message, which helped make some minor changes and got much better results. When tracking these results, the conversion is still one hundred percent, but the dollar value is still the highest and the leads are now into the double digits.

The other opportunity we saw in his KPI's was that one marketing campaign showed excellent lead generation, averaging over one hundred leads per month. However the conversion was low at eleven percent, and the dollar value was only two thirds of the value coming from the radio leads. To make improvements here, Danny began to focus on two fronts. He became more selective towards the type of leads he would chase from this source. He also focused more attention on following up his leads and convert them into paying customers. The result was a fifty three percent improvement in conversion. He levelled the value out to match the same average dollar value that radio is producing.

These improvements not only increased the level of work flowing through the business, but increased his profits by sixty four percent.

Remember, a copy of this spreadsheet is included as part of

the online course so make sure you get your copy by enrolling at **www.ProfitSecretRevealed.com**

Takeaways From This Chapter

- Measure the results from your all marketing campaigns, the conversion rates, average dollar sales
- Analyse your results at least monthly to chart your progress
- Remember to calculate your breakeven point so you know exactly how many sales you need to make from each marketing campaign
- Focus on improving your results

---

8 THE HIDDEN COST OF MARKETING

Thousands of books have been written on the subject of marketing and there are tens of thousands of people marketing themselves as gurus on the subject, as well as selling their marketing skills and services for you. However, very rarely have I read about or heard them talk about cost effective marketing or which are the least expensive strategies that will get you the fastest results. In fact, marketing is in itself of no value to you if you don't convert it into a sale. To ensure that you get the best results I recommend that you begin with some form of testing and measuring, before you begin marketing to guarantee that you will get a return on your investment.

There are hundreds of different strategies for sales and marketing, basically they can be grouped into the following categories: lead generation, conversion, average dollar sales and number of transactions per customer.

In order of least expensive strategies through to the most expensive, I would rank them in this order: conversion, average dollar sales, number of transactions and finally the most expensive, lead generation.

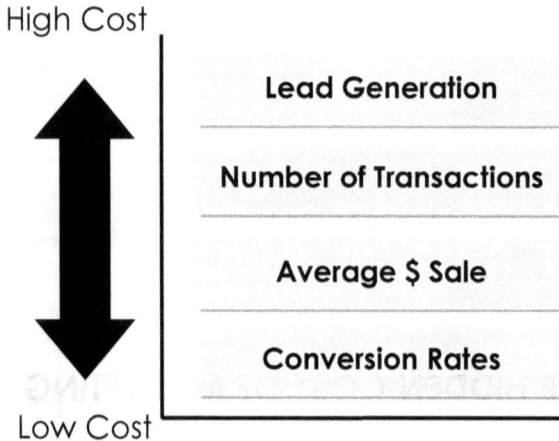

High Cost

| Lead Generation |
| Number of Transactions |
| Average $ Sale |
| Conversion Rates |

Low Cost

When reviewing your own KPI's for marketing, you should be mindful about the cost of certain strategies and if they will make any profitable improvement to your sales.

If one marketing campaign gives you plenty of leads, but the average dollar sale is low, you shouldn't consider increasing the marketing in an effort to make more money. Instead, you should think of ways to increase the average dollar sales with each of the customers from that campaign. Any strategy that you use to increase the average dollar spend from those customers will cost you a lot less than increasing your budget on that marketing campaign.

Examples of low to no cost strategies to increase your average dollar sales could include suggesting the most expensive item first. This could include making a three option close, offering package deals, or buying one to get the second half price. You could also sell service contracts or extended warrantees. There are many different ways to increase your dollar value. If you take the time to think about it, you will come up with some inventive ways to maximise the returns you get from your marketing dollar.

Likewise, you should always look at ways of improving your conversion. It will always be cheaper to convert the person in front of you than having to invest in more marketing to find another potential customer. It may be as simple as asking for the sale. Ask them, "how would you like to pay for that" (this will cost you absolutely nothing). You should also consistently follow up with people, this is the simplest of all strategies and will dramatically increase your number of leads converted.

I've heard many people say: "if only I had more customers". What they're really saying is: "I need more leads because I haven't converted the ones I've got". The key here is to start with your low hanging fruit. It always costs less to pick from the lowest branches. Never be fooled into thinking you need to spend more on marketing before you've learnt how to maximise the conversion of the potential customers right in front of you, if you don't follow this rule then you have the recipe for going broke, instead of the recipe for success.

Always remember: the majority of people want value for money and will pay a little more to get it. Only a few people truly want the absolute cheapest, so let them shop somewhere else.

Takeaways From This Chapter

- Focus on improving your conversion of your leads before increasing your marketing activity
- Look for ways to add value and up-sell your products and services to your customers
- Improve the conversion of your marketing campaigns before committing to spending more on other types of marketing

9 FOURTY EIGHT WAYS TO CUT EXPENSES & INCREASE YOUR PROFITS

1. **Simply increase your prices**
   It might be a scary prospect to increase your prices but just trust me, with the right attitude and sales script it will work.

2. **Focus on selling higher margin goods or services**
   If you couple this strategy with selling medium to high value items or services, you'll have the recipe to make more money while selling or doing less.

3. **STOP discounting**
   Discounting will cheapen your brand and kill your profitability so just STOP it

4. **Increase the quality of your products and service by having your own label or selling an exclusive label**
Selling higher quality or exclusive labels means one thing, higher mark up.

5. **Sack your C grade customers and focus on the A's and B's**
Focusing on your top spending, cash rich customers means you can focus more energy on up selling higher margin products to people who appreciate a value added experience and are willing to pay on time.

6. **Sell online**
If you're not already using the internet to generate sales then you're missing out on valuable customers and having the cheapest employee in your team (your online store) do the selling for you.

7. **Employ contractors and commission only sales people**
By employing contractors and commission only sales people you can massively reduce your fixed costs.

8. **Use cloud-sourcing for special projects and administration**
By utilising cloud-sourcing websites to employ people to do routine administration tasks, or one off projects such as graphic design or copy writing, you can save thousands of dollars as well as your valuable time.

9. **Train your staff in how to overcome objections**
The short term cost of training your staff in sales and overcoming objections will return you tens of

thousands of dollars, and you can be sure it will keep you ahead of your competition as well increasing your staff retention.

10. Reduce your team size and unnecessary management

No one likes to let people go but, if you need to reduce your team due to market conditions make sure you do it quickly and respectfully, to many businesses fail because they tried to hold on to excess people for too long, then everyone losses.

11. Have KPI's for efficiency, productivity and time management

Measuring departments and individual performance will empower you and your team to make better decisions about setting targets and implementing new strategies.

12. Renegotiate supplier agreements

Renegotiating terms of payment as well as reduced prices can free up vital cashflow and increase your margins.

13. Incentivise your staff and teach them to sell higher margin items

Incentivising people with monetary reward can work wonders for highly motivated people, try linking their bonuses to margins instead of the sale price and tell them which products have the highest margin.

14. Reduce double ups

By eliminating double ups you can reduce the costs of

both your sales and your fixed costs.

15. **Set monthly expenditure budgets and only allow your staff to buy with an authorised purchase order**
Implementing a system for ordering everything and anything for your business, from tea and coffee to stationary and materials, will prevent over stocking and double ups.

16. **Set a goal to reduce all expenses by ten percent**
It takes a team effort to reduce expenses so make sure you clearly communicate this goal.

17. **Eliminate re-works, do it right the first time**
Re-works cost businesses millions of lost profits every year, start by measuring the cost of re-works to your business then set some targets to reduce or totally eliminate all re-works, remember to clearly communicate this with all your team, and be prepared to reinforce your resolve.

18. **Recycle**
Recycling has been proven to save businesses in all industries money, recycling also adds a powerful cultural benefit to involve and inspire your staff and customers.

19. **Decrease your range or take stock on consignment to lower your cash that's tied up in inventory**
Selling off and deleting slow moving lines as well as decreasing your stock holdings will free up your cash reserves to invest into other areas of the business.

20. Measure stock turn and focus on selling your fastest moving stock

Focusing on and measuring stock turn for your highest moving stock will reduce cash that you've got tied up in slow moving items, and reduce your stock holding costs.

21. Buy in bulk for a discount, and pay and receive it from your supplier's overtime

In some situations it will make good business sense to buy stock on consignment for a discount and have your supplier warehouse it for you, this will reduce your costs and increase your margin.

22. Manufacture or import goods yourself

If you are a reseller of other peoples products, there will come a point in time you will have to move away from these suppliers and stock your own goods, this will dramatically increase your margin, be aware that your fixed costs will increase also to cover warehousing etc.

23. Promote idle time to customers and offer payment terms to receive overtime

A powerful strategy for manufactures to keep their equipment running 'around' the clock to maximise the returns on the equipment and reduce running costs.

24. Rent out or sub-let idle space

If you have a spare desk, office or storage space, you can potentially reduce your rent by thousands of dollars per year by sub-letting that space to another business.

25. Increase shifts to either two or three shifts

Another great strategy for manufactures. Increasing shifts will maximise your output of product without increasing your fixed costs, this will give you a greater return on your capital invested in equipment.

26. Use Time Tracking tools to avoid wasting time

For any business that trades time for money, it is essential that you track and measure every staff members time, failure to do so can have massive repercussions on your margins.

27. Join or start a buying group or co-operative

If you're a business that has good relationships with other businesses in your industry, you could start a buying group to import your own range of materials, products or components of what you sell. This will save you all money and increase your margins.

28. Re-structure your company debt

By reviewing and restructuring your company's debt, you can save thousands in interest payments every year. Make it a habit to review your banking, factoring and loan facilities every year.

29. Charge for a finance facility

If you are allowing your customers to purchase and pay over time, charge them interest and administration fees.

30. Reduce 30 day terms to 14 or 7 days or cash on delivery

Reducing your payment terms will increase the cash flowing into your business and save you interest on your overdraft facility.

31. Take deposits

It is common practice in all industries to accept deposits or payment up front, and your customer is conditioned to accept these terms so make sure you take the money now.

32. Invest in upgrading technology

Upgrading technology can make massive savings in many areas of your business. Do your research to find out how upgrades could benefit your business, set a budget and make an informed decision before you invest.

33. Automate as much as possible to reduce waste

Automation can be as simple as having timers on power or light switches and water taps, if you take the time to think about automation you could save a pile of money and help save the planet.

34. Sell obsolete equipment, as well as dead or old stock

Smart business owners know that only fools think obsolete equipment will make money or that old stock will sell... It won't so let it go, you'll be glad you did.

35. Move premises

Moving premises can have many positive spin offs including, being closer to, or more accessible to customers, giving you more or less space depending on your requirements, or even to gain a better quality work environment which can lift the productivity of your staff. Make sure you do your research and make a decision that best suits your business.

36. Pay cash rather than interest on debt

In order to conserve cashflow, avoiding debt is absolutely essential, especially on unnecessary purchases (like a flash car just to make yourself feel good) so where possible always pay cash.

37. Use a credit card for bonus points & up to 55 days interest free

Using credit cards can be a great way of delaying the payment of your bills to conserve your cashflow, but it is important that you pay your credit card bill in full and on time so you don't end up paying penalties and interest.

38. Rent for maximum tax write off

Renting your premises is in most cases one hundred percent tax deductible, unlike owning your own premises and paying principle and interest on the mortgage (only the interest can be deducted as an expense). Make sure you discuss your options with your accountant.

39. Keep overheads to a minimum

Successful business owners always keep an eye on their fixed expenses, however they also know that their true success lies in remembering to focus the majority of their efforts on margins.

40. Stop running marketing campaigns that don't work

The key is to know your break even on any marketing campaign and measure all your results, if the campaigns not working, fix it or dump it.

41. Measure everything

Nothing more to add to this as it sort of explains itself.

42. Check your utility bills for suppliers who might be over charging

I highly recommend that you never sign agreements with utility suppliers that lock you into fixed terms, especially for mobile phones. There are new deals and rates every month and if you're locked into a fixed term you will miss out on thousands of dollars of savings.

43. Change suppliers

If you're not getting a great service, a great deal and great payment terms, go and look for someone how will support your business with better deals and service.

44. Cut down on entertainment and travel costs

It is important that you set a budget for all entertainment and travel, and stick to it. A travel calendar is a great way to cut down on impulsive travel and should be planned out, three to six months in advance.

45. Upgrade the office electronics and make full use of cloud-based computing

Gone are the days of small businesses being held to ransom by big business costs, such as expensive software and onsite servers, if you need to upgrade then look at the many low to no cost options available to your business before taking the advice of a sales person with a narrow view and limited options.

46. Cut down on the amount of paper used to eliminate cost and inefficiencies

Cloud-based computing has given us the option of photographing or scanning all documents and storing them online, totally eliminating the paper war.

47. Re-examine your insurance coverage and policy costs

Just as you would with your banking and finance facilities, you should reassess your insurance needs every year. A good idea is to get at least two quotes from separate insurers.

48. Go green and install energy saving lighting and devises

Just like with automation of your energy systems, massive savings can be made by install energy efficient lighting and heating. Be careful to ensure that you maintain optimal lighting for your staff and customers. Bad lighting can reduce productivity and sales.

10 THE EASY WAY TO WRITE A BUDGET AND SET SALES TARGETS

One rarely used but powerful formula is the break-even formula. I've personally used it in many ways. I have used it to work out how much money a marketing campaign needs to generate in order to get a return on investment, or to set sales targets for a project or department. I have even used it to restructure entire business models. This formula, is also the basis behind working out annual budgets for a business.

It's a really nice, simple formula that includes two key components from your P&L, your margin and your expenses. I have probably never met a small business owner who consistently sits down and prepares an annual budget. If they have, I doubt it would be reviewed more than once a year.

A budget is important because it helps the business owner

set out three critical goals for the year: sales, expenses or controls on spending and, most importantly, profit. The smart business owner who is trained to be a great general manager of their business will make monthly reviews of the businesses actual performance or progress against this budget to keep their business on track and in line with their goals.

Most business owners, at some stage of their business, may have attempted to write a budget because they were told by their bank manager or accountant that it would be a good idea. They may have also read about it somewhere. However many business owners I've met have really struggled with the prospect of writing a budget, and most have abandoned the idea altogether.

When writing your budget, it's important to remember two key things. The first is that your budget is a goal for your business, and second is reviewing this goal monthly and comparing it with your actual results. Another thing to remember is that is easy to do, especially when you break it down into its three main parts: sales, expenses and profit. Before you even begin, please don't be put off by any past bad experiences. Remember to keep it simple.

To start preparing your budget, you need to know the break-even formula. The numbers you need for this formula are on your P&L. Remember: they are your margin and your expenses. The formula goes like this:

$$\text{Expenses} \div \text{Margin} = \text{Breakeven}$$

Let's use the numbers from Table1. in the chapter about Profit and Loss. The total expenses were $296,500 and the margin was 38% and with the break-even formula above, the answer would look like this:

$296,500 ÷ 0.38 = $780,263

So this business needs to make at least $780,263 in sales to break-even on all their expenses. Now it's important to note here that if there is a drop in margin, or an increase in expenses, then this breakeven sales amount will need to increase. If the margin increases or the expenses decrease, the value of the breakeven sales needed will decrease. Here's an example of a lower margin for let's say, 33%:

$296,500 ÷ 0.33 = $898,484

Or if the margin increased to 44%

$296,500 ÷ 0.44 = $673,863

Knowing this is all very well and good, but now you need to include some profit for your budget. Let's say, for instance, you'd like to make a profit of $100,000 this year. This becomes your goal and now you need to add it to your budget. All you need to do is add $100,000 to the break-even formula like this:

(Expenses + Profit) ÷ Margin = Sales Target
Or
($296,500 + $100,000) ÷ 0.38 = $1,043,421

Table 6

	Apr	May	Jun	Jul	Aug	Sep	Oct	Nov	Dec	Jan	Feb	Mar	Total
Sales	$ 90,000	$ 90,000	$ 75,000	$ 60,000	$ 55,000	$ 65,000	$ 80,000	$ 90,000	$ 125,000	$ 110,000	$ 108,000	$ 96,000	$ 1,044,000
COS	$ 55,800	$ 55,800	$ 46,500	$ 37,200	$ 34,100	$ 40,300	$ 49,600	$ 55,800	$ 77,500	$ 68,200	$ 66,960	$ 59,520	$ 647,280
GP	$ 34,200	$ 34,200	$ 28,500	$ 22,800	$ 20,900	$ 24,700	$ 30,400	$ 34,200	$ 47,500	$ 41,800	$ 41,040	$ 36,480	$ 396,720
Expenses	$ 24,708	$ 24,708	$ 24,708	$ 24,708	$ 24,708	$ 24,708	$ 24,708	$ 24,708	$ 24,708	$ 24,708	$ 24,708	$ 24,708	$ 296,500
Nett Profit	$ 9,492	$ 9,492	$ 3,792	-$ 1,908	-$ 3,808	-$ 8	$ 5,692	$ 9,492	$ 22,792	$ 17,092	$ 16,332	$ 11,772	$ 100,220

Table 5

	Apr	May	Jun	Jul	Aug	Sep	Oct	Nov	Dec	Jan	Feb	Mar	Total
Sales	$ 86,952	$ 86,952	$ 86,952	$ 86,952	$ 86,952	$ 86,952	$ 86,952	$ 86,952	$ 86,952	$ 86,952	$ 86,952	$ 86,952	$ 1,043,421
COS	$ 53,910	$ 53,910	$ 53,910	$ 53,910	$ 53,910	$ 53,910	$ 53,910	$ 53,910	$ 53,910	$ 53,910	$ 53,910	$ 53,910	$ 646,921
GP	$ 33,042	$ 33,042	$ 33,042	$ 33,042	$ 33,042	$ 33,042	$ 33,042	$ 33,042	$ 33,042	$ 33,042	$ 33,042	$ 33,042	$ 396,500
Expenses	$ 24,708	$ 24,708	$ 24,708	$ 24,708	$ 24,708	$ 24,708	$ 24,708	$ 24,708	$ 24,708	$ 24,708	$ 24,708	$ 24,708	$ 296,500
Nett Profit	$ 8,333	$ 8,333	$ 8,333	$ 8,333	$ 8,333	$ 8,333	$ 8,333	$ 8,333	$ 8,333	$ 8,333	$ 8,333	$ 8,333	$ 100,000

So now we have a set of goals to set out as our budget. Take the three numbers: expenses, profit and sales target, and divide them by twelve. Set them out in a monthly structure like this (Table 5) and add in the cost of sale and gross profit (just work this out as a percentage of the sales based on the margin i.e. COS would be sixty two percent of the sales):

It's as simple as that. This is the most basic format for a budget, but before you think the job is done, you need to do one more thing. You need to make some adjustments for seasonal changes in your business.

Every business goes through a summer and winter season. Sales for most businesses are at their highest during the summer and sales and activity drops away during the winter (please note that I don't mean the literal summer and winter of our physical seasons). An example of adjusting for the seasons might look like the one in Table 6.

Now you might notice that the business, in Table 6, slipped into three months of losses over July, August and September. This is normal for most businesses. The main thing is that you've budgeted for it. So, when winter arrives, it brings with it no surprises for you.

I will never forget the day I arrived at a client's office to find them celebrating a loss for that month. That may seem strange to you, but the fact was they had budgeted for a $25,000 loss that month and by comparing their budget to their P&L, they recorded a loss of less than half of what they had budgeted for. In other words, they had exceeded their goal and made more money than planned.

That brings me to another point about budgeting. As mentioned before, you must compare your actual performance to your budgeted performance. If you don't do this, there is no point in setting any goals for your business by preparing a budget. Your business will continue its aimless journey like a ship with no rudder.

Other uses for break-even include:

- Working out return on investment on marketing
- To set your prices
- To work out how many units you need to sell
- Work out if a product is viable
- Aids in preparing competitive bids or quotes
- Use when preparing information for loan applications
- Investing in new equipment or machinery
- To calculate the number of billable hours needed

11 LONG LIVE THE KING

Cash Is King. Yes it's an old expression and thrown around a lot, but it is an absolute, fundamental key to the survival and success of all businesses. Without cash flow, your business will die.

It is in fact possible for a business to survive on cash flow alone without being profitable. It's not much fun though; actually that situation can be downright miserable. On the other hand, profitable businesses without cash flow will not survive, period.

Success comes when you have both cash flow and profit. For many business owners, cash flow management looks something like this:

"What, another bill? How much money have we got in the

bank?"

And, when in they look at their bank account, they exclaim:

"Why hasn't this person paid us yet?"

If you're one of those business owners who look at their bank balance to decide whether or not to pay a bill, then you probably also suffer from a lot of sleepless nights. Let me make it perfectly clear that your bank balance is not a cash flow management system. Your bank account is merely a transactional facility for receiving and making payments.

If you're asking yourself why you should track your cash flow, let me give you some good answers to build up a case for doing so. Then I'll show you how and give you my rules for cash flow management. Cash flow forecasting will:

- Put you back in the driver's seat of your business
- Help you sleep at night
- Give you confidence in saying "We can pay you on the..."
- Make your creditors feel secure about when they'll get paid
- Help you collect money owed to you
- Give you a bigger picture of how your business is performing
- Show you where your money is going without referring to your P&L and Balance Sheet

There are many more reasons for having a cash flow system, but one of the keys you'll need to remember are frequency and consistency.

How often you prepare a cash flow forecast is entirely up

to you. There are hundreds, if not thousands of templates available for you to download from the Internet just by searching, "cash flow templates", but most of these are for annual forecasts.

Annual forecasts are fine, but if you're in a cash flow crisis, more commonly known as a cash gap, then an annual forecast isn't going to help put you back in control of your business or give you any great level of detail for daily or weekly spending. A cash flow forecast consists of your four main cash sources:

1. Income generated by the business (Sales)
2. Borrowed cash
3. Sale of assets
4. Or capital injection

And your six main uses;

1. General expenses
2. Purchase of fixed assets
3. Purchase of stock
4. Loan repayments
5. Owners drawings
6. Tax payments

Every business faces the dreaded cash gap from time to time. To help protect yourself from this nightmare and maximise your control over your business, I recommend doing weekly cash flow projection, six to eight weeks in advance. I say this because the majority of businesses have cash flowing in and out of the business on a daily or weekly basis. Therefore, it pays to know your cash position at all times.

Personally this is something I have my accounts staff do in any of my businesses. It gives me the greatest level of control over collecting and spending cash in my business.

When you join the free online course that accompanies this book at, **www.ProfitSecretsRevealed.com** you can download a spreadsheet version of the same eight week cashflow template that I use along with an instructional "how to" video.

Preparing a cash flow forecast is pretty simple. Start with your bank balance, add all the people who owe you money in the weeks that the amount is due, and then subtract all the amounts you owe to others on the weeks those bills fall due. This will leave you with a closing account balance for cash in the bank – plus or minus, at the end of each week.

You can then analyse your projections, and in the weeks where cash is tight, you can move some of your bill payments around in an attempt to stay cash positive. Some things to consider when preparing a cash flow forecast:

- You may have to make a rough guess to the amount that will be **coming in.**
- You may have to make a rough guess to the amount that will be **going out.**
- As you receive a payment or invoice, you can enter the **correct** amount.
- You can move your **cash out** amounts from week to week to achieve **positive** cash flow.
- Make sure you balance with your **bank statement** each week.

My golden rule for cash flow management is simple – No bills get paid without the cash flow forecast first being:

1. Updated from the previous week and all new cash in and cash out amounts added to the projection

2. Satisfactory answers to my questions about how much money we are likely to collect and, if it's a smaller amount, adjustments must be made to reflect this
3. Projection should be adjusted for any payment of bills I select, as well as moved to a later week for payment
4. Approved and signed off for payment by myself or a senior manager

After this is done – I mean, **only** after this is done, bills can be loaded for payment and payments made.

Other tips for managing your cash flow:
- Collect your money the majority of time.
- Review and change your trading terms.
- Have an efficient invoice system in place and send out regular statements.
- Monitor all your debtor and creditors.
- Be consistent in the follow up of anyone and everyone who owes you money (become a squeaky wheel).
- Only pay your bills on the last day of the terms, not before – it's a common mistake to pay bills or debts just because there's money in the bank, <u>always refer to your cash flow projections before paying any bills.</u>

12 CASH IN, CASH OUT – PURPOSE OF USING & UNDERSTANDING YOUR BALANCE SHEET

In many books about accounting, the chapter about Balance Sheets can make up half the book. The good news is I'm going to keep this chapter short and sweet, and focus on increasing just one thing, cash flow.

Cash flow is the heart beat of your business. As mentioned in the previous chapter, it is possible that a business will survive, even if it's bleeding profits, but having no cash flow is as fatal as having a heart attack.

There are three parts to your Balance Sheet: Assets, Liabilities and Equity. The first thing you must measure in your Balance Sheet is the sub-category of Assets called Current Assets. Current Assets include cash in your bank account, stock in your store or warehouse, and money owed to you by your debtors.

The type of business you operate determines which one of these you need to measure. If your business offers payment terms, you need to measure your Number of Debtor Days. If you, on the other hand, are a cash business and carry high levels of stock, you need to measure your Stock Turn. If you offer payment terms and you carry stock, then you need to measure both Debtor Days and Stock Turn.

The basic rule is, lower Debtor Days & higher Stock Turn the better your Cash "IN" Flow

Working Out Your Debtor Days

Most business owners tend to rely on using a report that is frequently called an "Aged Receivable" report. While this is a valuable report, telling you who owes you money and how much they owe you, it doesn't tell you how many days it takes on average to collect money.

By measuring and tracking your debtor days, you can collect valuable information about how your debt collections department is performing, even if that department consists of just one person, you.

To work out your debtor days, simply follow this flow chart and use the formula on the follow page.

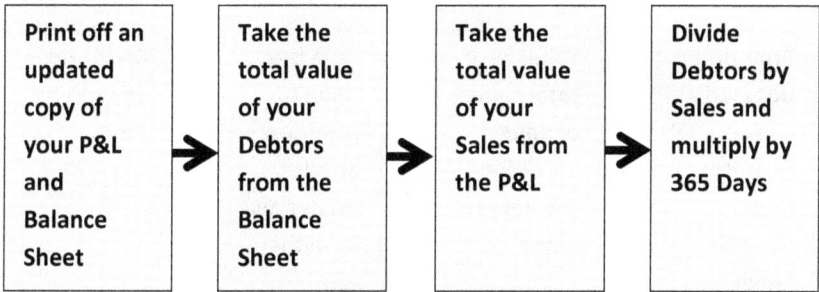

Print off an updated copy of your P&L and Balance Sheet	→	Take the total value of your Debtors from the Balance Sheet	→	Take the total value of your Sales from the P&L	→	Divide Debtors by Sales and multiply by 365 Days

$$Debtors \div Sales \times 365 = Debtor\ Days$$

With the numbers from our Balance Sheet (Table 7) and P&L (Table 1).

$$\$120,000 \div \$1,130,000 \times 365 = 38.7\ Days$$

Working Out Your Stock Turn

Carrying stock is a fine tuning act rather than a balancing act, it takes a fair amount of skill to identify what your customers are going to want to buy and how much stock to carry of that line. If you're not in the habit of measuring your Stock Turn then you run the risk of over ordering and carrying too much stock, that's to a lot of your cash invested in slow moving items or worse still, items that won't sell at all.

The other side of not knowing your Stock Turn, is under estimating how much stock you need to carry and seeing your customers take their cash to shop elsewhere because you've run out of the item they wanted to purchase.

Either scenario will lead to lower cash reserves in your business and your best line of defense is to measure your Stock Turn. To measure your Stock Turn, follow this flow chart and use the formula provided. Note that the Cost of Sale figure comes from the value of materials in the P&L (Table 1.).

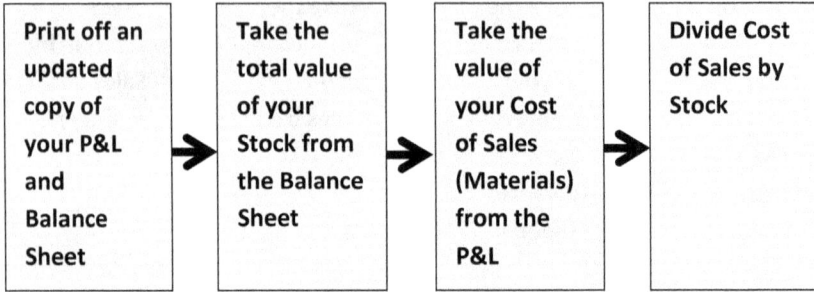

Print off an updated copy of your P&L and Balance Sheet	→	Take the total value of your Stock from the Balance Sheet	→	Take the value of your Cost of Sales (Materials) from the P&L	→	Divide Cost of Sales by Stock

Cost of Sales ÷ Stock = Stock Turn

Now include the numbers from the Balance Sheet (Table 7) and P&L (Table 1)

$340,000 ÷ $35,000 = 9.7 Turns of Stock Per Annum

First Steps To Increasing Stock Turn

1. Create an Inventory Management System

2. Measure Stock Turn

3. Offer only stock-high moving items

4. Sell down, auction, or dump obsolete stock

Ask yourself: what if …

1. We only sell high-end items?

2. Decrease our range?

3. Can we produce and sell our own label?

4. Can we secure and sell an exclusive label?

Then… move forward with a whole new Inventory Plan

Table 7
Balance Sheet for ABC Ltd March 2011

ASSETS

Current Assets

Bank	1,500
Debtors	120,000
Stock	35,000
	156,500

Fixed Assets

Motor Vehicles	185,000
Office Equipment	35,000
Plant	25,000
	245,000
Total assets	401,500

LIABILITIES

Current Liabilities

Creditors	78,000
GST	12,000
PAYE	10,000
Income Tax	42,500
	142,500

Long Term Liabilities

Bank Loan	25,000
Vehicle Finance	50,000
	75,000
Total Liabilities	217,500
Net Assets	184,000

EQUITY

Retained earnings	174,000
Current earnings (net profit)	10,000
	184,000

Here are thirty two great strategies I've used in the past to improve cashflow

1. Have a cash plan for your business

It is hard to improve your cash position if you don't know where you're at.

2. **Chase your money**

   There is no excuse for not getting on the phone and following up of money that's owed to you.

3. **Eliminate invoicing delays**

   It is an absolute must to get your invoicing done and dispatched as soon as possible.

4. **Request progress payments on large orders**

   It's common practice to request deposits and progress payments, spell out the time line and terms for payment before you sell your product service.

5. **Time your invoices to coincide with your customer's payment schedule**

   Make sure you know your customers cut off point for receiving invoices, missing the deadline can result in serious delays in receiving your payment

6. **Grant cash discounts to key accounts**

   You can offer small discounts to some key customers to reward them if they pay on time, the opposite of this strategy is to add penalties or interest to bad payers bills. Please note, this is a different strategy to giving an upfront discount just to make the sale, this discount is to get the money, in some cases I'd sooner give a small discount to get $95.00 now rather than wait sixty or more days to get $100.00.

7. **Increase selling prices after evaluating volume considerations**

   Just like with margins, increasing your prices can improve your cash position, this strategy works well for cash businesses like retailers.

8. **Negotiate special payment terms with key suppliers**
Renegotiate with your suppliers to extend your payment terms, the longer the terms the better.

9. **Set up a payment schedule for large payables**
If you've gotten behind with your suppliers account, negotiate a payment plan that you can both agree on and keep to your agreement.

10. **Use extended payment plans for business insurance premiums**
Paying insurance premiums up front can mean paying less but sometimes, it makes more sense to forego the discount and hold onto your cash reserves and pay over time.

11. **Negotiate billing dates that coincide with publication dates of large ad campaigns**
Never pay for advertising up front, request that the publisher of the campaign set up an account for you so you can make payment after the ads have run and you've had a chance to convert the leads to sales to pay for the advert.

12. **Have retainers and payment terms with sub-contractors that correspond with the terms you have with your customer**
Where possible make sure your payment terms for contractors follow your payment terms with your customers. Be sure to check you legal obligations and stay within the law.

13. **Use the internet to obtain competitive prices and renegotiate with current suppliers**

    Do your research to make sure you're not being charged more than what your suppliers competition are offering.

14. **Pay for large service contracts over the life of the contract**

    Make payment terms over the full term, some suppliers will try and get payment upfront or in a shorter term. (e.g. Yellow Pages run for a full 12 months but will try and make the payment terms over three to six months.)

15. **Use automated payment systems to schedule payment on the exact due date**

    Internet banking allows you to set up payments in advance, never pay before you need to. Set and forget.

16. **Adopt a "just in time" inventory system for key items**

    If you can trust your supplier to meet your schedules, then place orders with them on an "as and when needed" basis instead of holding and paying for their stock.

17. **Defer fixed asset additions**

    If you don't need to upgrade your equipment, don't go and buy it just because "you'd like to have it".

18. **Set up a cash drop system for cash receipts**

    Have a cash limit in your till and drop the excess cash into your safe at regular intervals to prevent theft or losses

19. Negotiate contract term loans with your bank

In certain cases you can apply for a special purpose loan that is tied to the terms of large contracts with unique payment terms.

20. Tie a short-term loan to a future cash inflow

For countries that have user pays tax duties like GST, VAGST or VAT, use the tax refund from a large purchase to pay back the loan.

21. Consider factoring accounts receivable

If your margin allows it, you could "sell" a selection of your invoices to a factoring company to free up cashflow on slow payers. Note: Don't use this option on bad debts.

22. Avoid cash travel advances for employees

Reimburse on actual expenditures instead. If an employee doesn't have a credit card and they travel often, offer to reimburse the annual fee. Don't use company credit cards.

23. Only pay bonuses in high seasons

Schedule annual bonuses, profit sharing and dividend payments during seasonal periods of high cash in-flows.

24. Change payrolls from weekly to fortnightly or monthly

Delaying payroll payments will conserve your cash reserves and reduce administration.

25. **Delay payroll by five to seven days after end of pay period**

It is common practice to pay employees after the period worked, don't succumb to the temptation of paying for the week worked in the same period, payment should made be in the following work period.

26. **Evaluate the cash impact of owning company cars vs. reimbursing employees for business use of their cars**

Doing this exercise could free up tens of thousands of dollars of capital.

27. **Reduce loans to staff**

Make it company policy to refuse cash advances on a staff members wages and make loans top staff tougher to get with a full application and credit history process.

28. **Liquidate obsolete or unusable inventory**

If it's not selling, let it go and get whatever price you can for it, sometimes it's better to cut your losses and move onto better, faster moving stock.

29. **Sell non-productive assets**

If it's inefficient, unreliable or just worn out – sell it.

30. **Consider sale and leaseback arrangements**

If you have equity in your assets, you can sell them to a finance company and then lease them back to free up your equity.

31. **Institute a company-wide inventory reduction program**

Make sure your staff know that their role includes ensuring no one over orders and all stock must move quickly.

32. **File Goods and Services taxes on a cash basis if you meet the requirements**

Talk to your accountant or tax agent to see if you qualify for moving from an invoice basis to cash basis on certain tax types.

13 BONUS CHAPTER – DEBT COLLECTION SYSTEM

STEP 1. Reduce terms and review conditions

- No more end of month statements – they cost you time, money and resources, and are not necessary.
- Terms Cash on Delivery, 7 or 14 days, invoiced at the time of delivery (No matter the time of the month).
- "A" grade customers may have 30 days if necessary
- Remember – if a B, C or D grade customer is worried about your terms, they are usually **not** worried about **when** they have to pay, but rather **how** they are going to pay. If this is the case you have to ask yourself, "Are they a **bad** credit risk?"
- Remember – Utilities such as phone, water etc. are pay on invoice only (no statements are issued). They will cut off your service if you don't pay. People tend to pay these bills first, so why not be like them.

STEP 2. Choose the team member responsible

- Stress the importance of the role and its necessity to be done as a continual process
- Promise to support them
- Set and agree on their targets e.g. number of calls per day, amount collected per week...

STEP 3. Have a clear "Aged Receivables" report

- Any good accounting software or trade designed software will have this function
- This report will show the accounts overdue and by how much. Often they are defaulted at Current (0 – 30), 30 – 60 days, 60 – 90 days and greater than 90 days. Set the report to match your terms
- Have this report printed at **least weekly** (if not daily) by the person responsible
- Set targets. For example: over a period of time, how many accounts are overdue in each category and the amount acceptable (obviously 0 is the target however, it takes time to reduce the list)

STEP 4. Be prepared

- Have all the information you need. Amounts, invoice numbers (or a copy of the invoice), contacts, notes from previous calls etc.
- Make detailed notes of any conversations and promises: names, dates, times, what was promised etc.
- Pick a time, daily or weekly, for the calls to be made – block out the time. No interruptions.

STEP 5. Set your rules

- Know exactly what to say:

- Develop a script for each call
- Develop a standard letter for sending after 3 calls

STEP 6. Set the tone

- Always use the 3 "F's" – FIRM, FAIR & FRIENDLY (You catch more flies with honey than you do with vinegar!)
- Stick to facts. Don't get into an emotional argument. If the customer becomes heated, rude or abusive, exit the call (sometimes this may even mean hanging up) and refer the problem to the Owner/Manager.
  - Your team members are not being paid to be abused – they are just doing a job.
    - You must ring up and challenge this person ASAP.
    - Insist on an apology to your team member.
  - You must support your team.
  - To avoid this problem in the future, you may need to change these particular customers terms to COD or choose not to deal with them at all.

STEP 7. Follow the contact schedule

- Consistency of contact is the key – the squeaky wheel gets the oil
- Do what you promise

STEP 8. Don't avoid the problem.

- Get on with it
- Remember under contract law that at the time of sale, they have agreed to pay for your product or service on the terms you specified. If they haven't, they have broken the contract.

- Some clients may be under significant financial pressure, either on a personal or business front. A payment solution may need to be arranged:
    - The client needs to admit they need help to pay.
    - The right blend of empathy and responsibility is needed.
    - Get the payment plan in writing and signed off by both parties.
    - It is better to help someone through and be paid than to alienate them and not be paid.
- At a certain stage of the process, (usually after the third call) be prepared to put the customer on "**stop supply**".
    - Enforce it!
    - Do not allow customers to rack up more debt if they are bad payers – teach them your way of doing business.
    - Note: it is surprising how many businesses will pay the bill when they need something.
    - Never tell the gatekeeper or the counter jockey they are on stop supply.
        - Always inform the owner or those responsible for accounts payable.
        - If more orders are placed with you, phone the person who placed the order and inform them you are unable to supply and they should talk to the manager.

STEP 9. Review

- Regularly review the call sheets and identify businesses that are habitual bad payers.
    - Put them on **cash on delivery** or at least reduce their terms.
    - Choose **not** to deal with them.

ACTION Points
Call 1.
- Two days after overdue (to allow for mail)
- Eighty percent of overdues will be paid due to oversight or the fact that you have rung.

Call 2.
- One week after first call (nine days overdue).
- This call is important in that it shows you are on the ball and not going away.
- Always go over what was said in the previous call and what they promised to do (This puts you in control, and the customer feeling guilty for being caught out).

Call 3.
- One week after the second call (16 days overdue), or no later than two days after they promised an action (eg. I will do a bank transfer tonight).
- Put them on "stop supply" if necessary and inform them it will be lifted as soon as payment is received.
- Always go over what was said in the previous calls and what they promised to do (This puts you in control, and the customer feeling guilty for being caught out).
- Ask if there is any problem with the payment.
  - Brings any problems to a head and also challenges them not to lie.
  - If there is a problem refer to the manager regarding a repayment plan.

Letter To Client
- One week after third call.
- Outline contacts and failure of commitments made on

previous dates.

- Stress they already are on "stop supply."
- State that if payment is not made or if you have not heard from them by a certain date, the matter will be passed to your debt collection agency.
  - Allow time for post, weekends, and a few days to organise themselves.

Send Matter to Collection Agency

- If by this stage they have failed to deliver on promises and failed to react to the letter, resolve the matter – don't stuff around anymore!
- It is better to get eighty percent of what your owed now, rather than zero – at least you can cover for your costs and keep the cash flowing forward.
- Some debt collecting agencies add their fees to the amount so you are not out of pocket.
- Once at this stage the matter is resolved and not a source of lingering annoyance for the owner – a real source of stress.

Black List or Full Payment Up Front

Choose not to deal with the customer or at most full payment up front – don't get caught again! If you choose the Payment Up Front method of dealing with this customer, add on twenty percent or more to their list price.

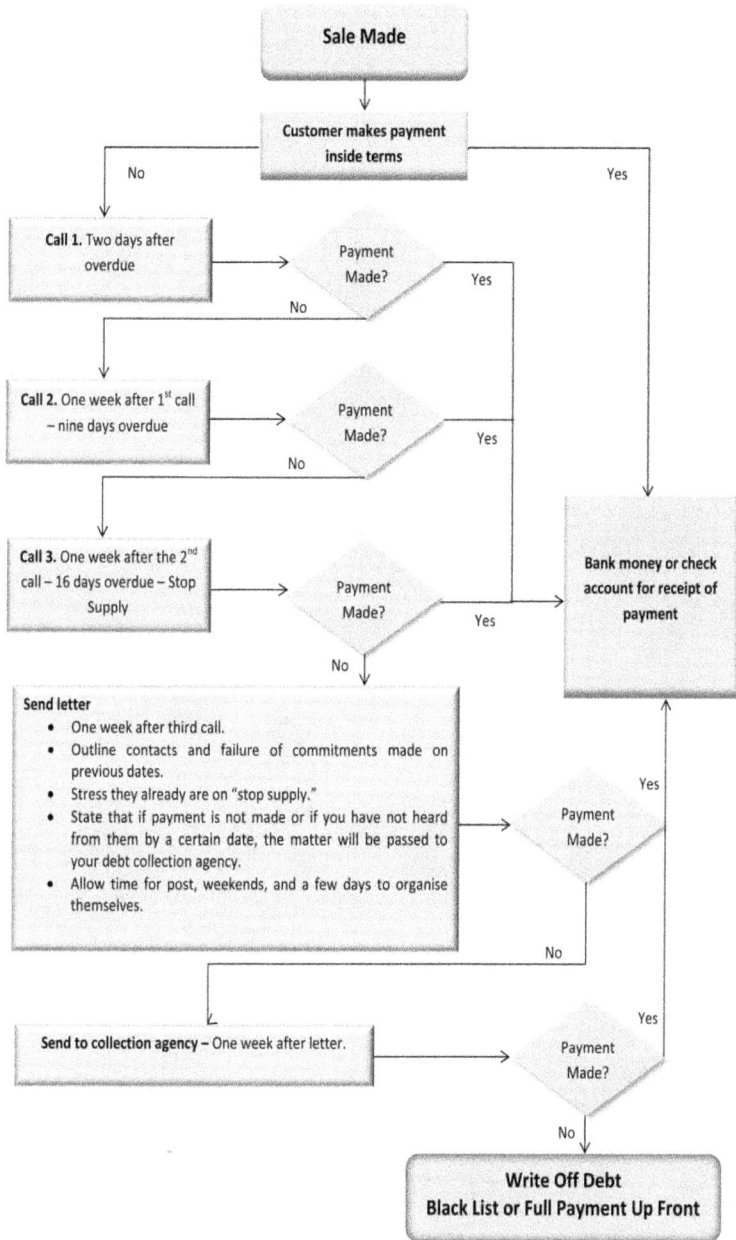

```
                          ┌─────────────────┐
                          │    Sale Made    │
                          └────────┬────────┘
                                   │
                                   ▼
                     ┌─────────────────────────┐
        ┌────────────┤ Customer makes payment   ├────────────┐
        │     No     │      inside terms         │    Yes     │
        │            └─────────────────────────┘             │
        ▼                                                     │
┌──────────────────┐         ◇ Payment                       │
│ Call 1. Two days  ├───────►   Made?  ──── Yes ──┐           │
│ after overdue     │            No               │           │
└────────┬─────────┘             │                │           │
         │                       │                │           │
         ▼                       │                │           │
┌──────────────────┐         ◇ Payment           │           │
│ Call 2. One week  ├───────►   Made?  ──── Yes ──┤           │
│ after 1st call –  │            No               │           │
│ nine days overdue │             │                │           │
└────────┬─────────┘             │                │           ▼
         │                       │                │   ┌──────────────────┐
         ▼                       │                │   │ Bank money or     │
┌──────────────────┐         ◇ Payment           │   │ check account for │
│ Call 3. One week  ├───────►   Made?  ── Yes ────┴──►│ receipt of        │
│ after the 2nd     │            No                   │ payment           │
│ call – 16 days    │             │                   └──────────────────┘
│ overdue – Stop    │             │                            ▲
│ Supply            │             ▼                            │
└──────────────────┘                                          │
```

Send letter

- One week after third call.
- Outline contacts and failure of commitments made on previous dates.
- Stress they already are on "stop supply."
- State that if payment is not made or if you have not heard from them by a certain date, the matter will be passed to your debt collection agency.
- Allow time for post, weekends, and a few days to organise themselves.

◇ Payment Made? — Yes ──► (to Bank money or check account for receipt of payment)

No

Send to collection agency – One week after letter. ──► ◇ Payment Made? — Yes ──► (to Bank money or check account for receipt of payment)

No

┌──┐
│   Write Off Debt   │
│ Black List or Full Payment Up Front   │
└──┘

ABOUT THE AUTHOR

Matt Jull started his career as an apprentice in the building industry. At the age of 20, with a $300 loan from his father, he started his own business.

In six months, he had 20 staff working for him and then realised he knew "bugger all" about running a business. Six months later, he sacked them all to start afresh.

Matt says, "I realised very quickly that, although I knew how to be a great tradesman, my training had not prepared me to be a business owner. Therefore, I let go of my ego, downsized, and started over. I then set about learning how to run a successful and profitable business from scratch."

His first step towards success was to engage a business coach who taught him Bucky Fuller's teachings on generalised principles. These principals affect everything from who we are to what we do. Most importantly, I AM responsible for what happens in my business. Too many business owners have found someone or something to hang blame on and continue to use this as a crutch by piling up the excuses for why they are who they are.

Matt was also fortunate enough to be mentored by Barry Dow, a millionaire business owner, CEO, turnaround specialist, and mentor. Barry trained Matt in the principles of turnaround management and company restructuring.

Matt's approach to business growth is to first tackle instability by delving into profit ratios, cashflow, and people issues, and then pursue any form of growth strategies, such as sales and marketing.

Matt says, "If there is no profit margin in what you're selling, or there are major cashflow issues in the back end of your business, these problems will be magnified 100 fold by increasing sales through marketing and putting more stress on the business and its owners. The first step for any business owner is to understand how to make a profit, perfect their pricing strategy and maximise cashflow before implementing any clever marketing strategies."

Matt's methods are laid out in the four stages discussed in this book and are under pinned by General Management Best Practice and Generalised Principles.

These methods have produced many award-winning businesses. Matt's clients have won awards for: Best Marketing, Best Team, Best Franchise System, Best Franchisee,

Best Customer Service, Best Overall Award, Best Customer Service and Supreme Business Award.

Matt's passion and expertise leads him to work with many different industry groups and businesses ranging in size from 2 – 3 employees to over 200 employees, as well as turnovers from the high $100,000's to over $200 million.

Matt lives in Auckland, NZ with his wife Harriet and four his sons, Ethan, Jackson, Theo and Edward. Matt divides his time between his family, coaching junior rugby, and frequent trips to visit his interests in the South Pacific.